From a New Forest Inclosure

Book Four 2010 &2011

By

Ian Thew

Published by Burley Rails Publishing
Burley Rails Cottage BH24 4HT

ISBN 978-0-9570835-3-0

Ian Thew

Born in Southampton, Ian and his siblings were brought, throughout their childhood, into the New Forest to walk and enjoy the open space. Although, initially, he spent his adult life living and working away from  the Forest he was always keen on the countryside and country sports, especially fishing and shooting. He returned whenever he could to the Forest until, eventually, he settled down in Burley with his late wife, Diane. In 1994 they moved to the remote Burley Rails Cottage which, originally built as a woodman's cottage and sold by the Forestry Commission in the 1960's, is a unique place in which to live.

Ian's knowledge of the forest is genuine and he is respected for his considerate and well researched articles which are published in national and international magazines. These booklets have been produced with the encouragement of readers who wished to refer to a particular article which had been lost in a discarded magazine and at the suggestion of those who wanted friends, relatives and visitors in general to understand the Forest and its ways. So whether a Villager, Visitor, Tourist, or Grockle, whatever your guise, we hope these snippets will help you to understand what is so very special about this wonderful place.

Book Four in the 'From a New Forest Inclosure' series is an anthology of the articles which were written by the author in 2010 and 2011 for the Burley Village magazine.   These light-hearted and informative observations were made in the most part from his home deep within a New Forest Inclosure.

Explore these pages and chuckle at more tales from the Royal Oak and the antics of the spoilt pony; read about the squirrel's tail, Country Watch, the village show and discover how Obi-Wan Kenobi came to the Forest!

Ian Thew

January

Now that the Christmas festivities are just a memory it's a good time to reflect upon the past year. Up here in the Inclosure I've met people from all walks of life; some pleasant and some not so pleasant, some I've already told you about in my past ramblings but there are others who, for one reason or another, deserve a mention.

Back in the summer I was on the bridge just below the house, I'd gone down to the river to find some respite from the sweltering, midday heat. On the wooden handrail I'd spotted a beautiful brown and green lizard that lay basking in the sunshine and, as I stood admiring it, an elderly couple approached from the direction of Anderwood. The man had a camera dangling from a wrist strap and without a word I pointed to the lizard.

Common Lizard

His face lit-up and he quickly took a few snaps of the reptile before it took fright and disappeared, as only a lizard can. It was only then that we spoke; he asked me if I knew where I was. I replied in the affirmative and he went on to explain that he and his wife had travelled down from London in order to take a stroll around our beautiful Forest and now they were hopelessly lost. Not only were they lost but it was obvious that they were both very concerned by their predicament and extremely tired too.

So, without further ado, I walked them slowly back to the house, gave them a drink and drove them back to their car. Not so unusual you might think? But read on, for in the post, a few days later, I received a letter of thanks from the couple and, enclosed with it, was a photo of that stunning lizard – now, in this day and age when good manners seem so rare, that was unusual! But wasn't it nice?

My next encounter was not so pleasant but not without its funny side either. I was in my workshop changing a fluorescent light tube when I heard a terrible commotion from outside. From the sound of things my Jack Russell was living up to his breeds' reputation! Without thinking, I hurried through the gate still clutching the blown light tube and encountered a very agitated young man who was clearly dressed for running and with raised foot, was about to kick my dog! Naturally I advised him, in the nicest possible terms, that he might regret his intended action. He looked-up and explained in vociferous and graphic terms that my Jack had taken a bite out of one of his three dogs which, as he spoke, were snapping and snarling around his legs. I said that I felt sure that his dog was sorry that it had been bitten but added that it probably deserved it. I went on to explain that my dogs were all working dogs and would not fight unless provoked. He didn't appreciate my response and made a move towards me; for a moment I thought he was going to attack me and, without thinking, I raised my hand – yes, the hand that was clutching a four foot long fluorescent tube! He stopped in his tracks, eyed the tube and then turned tail and trotted off down the road calling his dogs as he went. I thought no more of the incident but later on I related the tale to a friend who found the whole thing highly amusing.

"Don't you see it" he said "an old man in the woods with a 'lightsabre' he probably thought he'd encountered Obi-Wan Kenobi from Star Wars!"

May the Force be with you and have a happy and prosperous new year.

February

Another Christmas and New Year have come and gone. Gone too, back to their own homes, are the Children, the Grandchildren, the In-laws, the Out-laws and all the other guests who came to help with the celebrations. Gone too, thank goodness, is the last of the Turkey; personally, I'm glad that Christmas only comes but once a year –there's only so much turkey and turkey soup that a man can cope with! The decorations have been taken-down, packed into boxes and stacked on the landing beneath the attic into which they are destined to reside for another year when, that is, someone can work up the enthusiasm and the courage to brave entry into that freezing part of the house! In the fruit bowl one or two desiccating oranges have survived the Christmas feast whilst in the fireplace a few charred nut shells peep through the ashes of the yuletide logs. Outside a once resplendent and bedecked Christmas tree, now naked and forlorn, together with few holly boughs whose once resplendent, red berries are now shrivelled and paled, are lying in anticipation of their ultimate end - on the first bonfire of 2010.

New Year is a time for new beginnings and a time for resolutions and so, determined to start the year in the manner that I had resolved should continue, I braved the cold morning of the first Monday in January and, bedecked in my clumsy, protective clothing, I set-off with a chain-saw to cut-up a fallen tree for next winters' fuel supply. And then, without warning and without consideration to my new-found, good intentions, it snowed! And oh boy, did it snow? Now don't get me wrong, I'm not a wimp, but swinging around on the end of a heavy chainsaw whilst the snow is falling thick and fast is not my idea of fun! It soon became very slippery underfoot and thus dangerous, so, letting discretion overcome valour, I retired to the crossword, a glass of amber liquid and a roaring log fire.

I arose early (well, early-ish!) on Tuesday morning and looked out onto a transformed Forest. Anxious to go and investigate, I fed the dogs, filled the nut feeders and whizzed-up a good bowlful of bread crumbs for the bird table and then, chores completed, I wrapped-up and set-off into a wondrous, new Inclosure.

All around the front gate, the tracks of Charlie fox, clearly distinguished by the occasional imprint of his brush, were in abundance; as was the single-file spoor of a fallow deer and everywhere were the side-by-side footprints of birds that hop in order to get around. I spotted the 'two forward-two behind' prints of a rabbit, an unusual sight in this neck of the woods, which encouraged me to follow them to see where they went. They took me to the main Bolderwood–Burley track where something even more unusual and sinister took my attention. There, in the snow, right in the middle of the track, were a few drops of bright, red blood! A few paces further there were more and then still more again, as I followed the road towards Burley. For a while I was puzzled, for there were no animal tracks to be seen; so where had the blood come from? So intent was I on following the blood spoor that I had failed to notice the clean set of wheel tracks that ran either side of it. Then all became clear; a vehicle carrying a freshly-killed beast had driven past, thus leaving the tell tale drops. But was it a Keeper going about his legitimate business or was it someone up to no good?

Snow good worrying about it!

Snow changes everything

March

I know I'm always banging-on about squirrels but quite frankly I don't like them! As far as I'm concerned they are non-indigenous, destructive varmints that should never have been introduced to this country. However, I'm sure that many will disagree with me and that's okay; after all, we're all entitled to our own opinion.

Just recently the subject of squirrels was raised during a discussion I was having with a retired keeper who lives on the other side of the Forest. He told me a tale which highlights the difference of opinion that we can all have where wild animals are concerned and I think it's worth repeating.

Imagine if you can the New Forest in the early Fifties when things were so very different; tourism was in its infancy and cars were a luxury shared by few. It was about 10.00 o'clock and the keeper had just arrived home for his mid-morning break when the phone began to ring. It was Lymington police station and the sergeant on the other end of the line asked if he could take care of an injured squirrel. Now, controlling squirrels was a major part of the keepers' job and his initial response to this strange request was not for the pages of this genteel magazine. The sergeant calmed him down and assured him that the request was genuine and would he please help him out by taking care of this squirrel that a concerned visitor had brought into the station. Reluctantly the keeper agreed and in due course a well dressed gentleman carrying a cardboard box emerged from a long, gleaming motor car that had pulled up at his door. The man was clearly distraught as he handed him the box and pleaded with him to 'do what he could for the poor little animal inside'.

On opening the box the keeper found one of his arch-enemies neatly wrapped in a very smart sweater. He remarked that there didn't seem to be a lot wrong with it and the gentleman explained that it had indeed taken him and his companion, who had driven over for the day from Portsmouth, some time to catch it. The keeper enquired after the whereabouts of his companion and was surprised to learn that he was in Lymington hospital where, having been badly bitten by the said squirrel, he was being treated for his injuries!

The keeper was in a dilemma; he had a reputation for speaking his mind and was inclined to tell the gentleman just what he thought of him and his friend but something in the man's' demeanour made him hold his tongue and, without further ado, he agreed to 'look after' the squirrel and sent him on his way.

The keeper was good at his job and proud of the reputation he had for keeping these grey invaders under control so, as soon as the car disappeared from view, he quickly dispatched the injured squirrel and being a thrifty man and not one to waste anything, he fed it to his ferrets and went back to his work.

Early the next morning there was another knock on his door and on opening it the keeper was surprised to find the same agitated gentleman on his threshold. The man explained that he was worried about the squirrel and, after a sleepless night, he had driven over from Portsmouth to enquire after its well being. The keeper was now in more of a dilemma and taking the man's arm he steered him back towards his car explaining that it was pity that he hadn't arrived earlier for, having nursed the squirrel all night, he had released it not ten minutes ago 'and what a joy it was to see the little fellow as it bounded through the trees'. And all the time he prayed that the man wouldn't turn round and spot the bushy tail that protruded through the wire of the ferrets' hutch!

It takes all sorts – thank goodness!

Shot squirrel retrieved by Jack

April

What an awful winter we've had! It's been the topic of discussion on more than one occasion and most people that I've met have assured me that it's been the longest winter of their lives; but now, at last, there is a hint that things just might be on the change. It's now mid March and until recently the Forest and, especially my padocks, could best be described as sodden. Unfortunately, I had urgent fencing repairs which could not be delayed, so I just had to grit my teeth and struggle in the cloying mud that sucked at the boots and wrenched my aged knees with every step. The temperature didn't help either – it's been unseasonably cold up here in the Inclosure with, it seemed, every daybreak revealing a frosted lawn and frozen pond. But, as always, just when you're beginning to wonder if it will ever end, there comes a time when someone 'up there' decides that we've had enough and throws the magic switch.

Suddenly the rain stopped, the Sun began to show some enthusiasm for life and the wind came out to play and, between them, they began to warm and dry the miserable soil. Snowdrops popped out to see what all the fuss was about and were closely followed by an occasional crocus and then more and more of them until great swathes of colour now cheer-up our once, dreary gardens. The daffodils have shown more caution – yes, they're up and in bud too, but it's not quite warm enough for them to work up the courage and open their beautiful yellow heads – or, perhaps, they know something that the others don't?

In the kitchen garden the rhubarb has poked its head out to see what's going on but the broad beans have decided that discretion is the better part of valour and are resolutely refusing to make an appearance. The onion sets and the shallots are inactive but, surprisingly, their Mediterranean cousin, the garlic, has defied the cold weather and produced some spectacular shoots.

The birds too are beginning to notice the change in seasons. The chiff-chaff, that harbinger of spring, has been heard on more than one occasion and the great-spotted woodpeckers are drumming away in the warming sunshine. In deference to this sudden change-of-heart by 'He who controls the weather' I took the trouble to clean-out the old nesting boxes and gave thought to making some more. I was sure that it would not be too late to site more nest boxes - but perhaps I was wrong; for just yesterday I found, on the driveway, the pathetic corpses of three, newly-fledged bluetits that, clearly, were hatched too early.

The bird table and feeding stations are smothered by a continually changing swarm of birds and I'm hard-pushed to keep them topped-up. In fact, I gradually realised that I was filling the wire cages more frequently than ever and, on closer investigation, I discovered that someone or something had paid a visit with what must have been a set of wire cutters! For there, at the base of each feeder, one or two strands of the mesh had been cut; thus creating a hole large enough to remove a whole peanut. I spent a while watching the birds coming and going but never saw one with anything that resembled a tool bag! It wasn't until early the next morning, when I looked out from my bedroom window, that I discovered the culprit. There clinging to the wire basket was a squirrel -now I know I'm continually banging on about my arch-enemies but this was just not fair - there it was, neatly modifying my property, with its enormous incisors! But not for long!

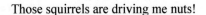

Those squirrels are driving me nuts!

Blue Tit

May

According to the Chinese, we are in the year of the Tiger. Now, if I could have my way, I'd definitely say we were in the year of the Toad and I'll tell you why. The recent, warming temperatures coupled with unprecedented rainfall have encouraged a migration of toads, across the Forest, of a magnitude that hasn't been witnessed for many a year. Toads usually emerge from hibernation in late February and are immediately driven by a primeval urge to return to their birth-place where they will ensure the continuation of their species. But this year, this annual, dogged, often epic pilgrimage, back to the pond or lake where they were born, occurred later than is normal - probably because of the unusually low temperatures that we experienced in January and February – however, any adverse effects that this late start may have caused have been compensated by sheer numbers. I really can't remember seeing such vast quantities of toads as I have witnessed this year.

On a day in late March I went to christen a new fly rod and, as I stalked carefully around the lake, I spotted a toad in the shallow margins, which I was delighted to see. I stopped to examine the amphibian and, a few feet from it, I noticed another then I became aware of another and then another. It soon became apparent that the lake was harbouring a huge abundance of toads- there were toads everywhere; some motionless on the bottom of the lake; some moving purposefully and others, just visible, skulking, in the deeper water. Catching the newly-stocked trout, which was the purpose of my visit, suddenly became insignificant and fly fishing lost its usual attraction as I quickly became absorbed by this amazing spectacle that I was privileged to be witnessing. I completed a circuit of the lake trying to count the number of toads, but it was an impossible task for the male toad is a tenacious lover, (albeit easily confused) and I frequently found the much larger, female toad with a smaller male clamped firmly on her back and, occasionally, a similar duo with an additional male clamped onto the male below! A female toad will wander around for hours or sometimes days, carrying her paramour with her and, as I've already suggested, the male toad is easily confused and it's not uncommon to find one misguidedly locked onto a large, rounded pebble or, as I once encountered another, resolutely fastened across the head of a large and clearly perplexed koi carp!

At one end of the lake the waters were swarming with mating toads and there, among them, I spotted some toad spawn, which differs from the familiar 'tapioca' of frog spawn insomuch as it's produced in long strings. I reached into the water and gently lifted one of these gelatinous ropes which, being tangled in a mass of toads and yet more spawn, refused to be raised more than an inch or two. The numbers of toads and the massive volumes of spawn production were awesome and to say that there were thousands of these warty amphibians would not be an exaggeration.

I phoned the fishery manager, a man who has been working around this particular water for many years, to report my discovery. He informed me that the lakes had always been home to a substantial number of toads and

went on to say that because he'd been rather puzzled by their absence he'd been keeping an eye out for them and, it was only yesterday that he'd spotted the first arrivals but no more than ten individuals! So there you are, what miracle, this plethora of amphibians had walked into the lake unnoticed by all, under cover of darkness, in less than twenty-four hours!

Must go now before you all 'croak' with boredom!

Trout Lake

June

Here we are in the middle of May and frost warnings are still being issued by the Met Office but, to compensate for some occasional chilly nights, we have been blessed with warming sunshine during the day. Both the garden and the surrounding Forest were reluctant to make a spring-time effort, but now, at last, our little part of the world is a beautiful place. A wall of green has descended on my boundaries which increases the impression of total seclusion and, indeed, the illusion of increased protection from the troubles of the outside world. What a privilege it has been when, puzzled and concerned by the recent debacle of the election, I was able to wander down through the garden and enjoy the peace and tranquility that it instills.

People often ask if I ever feel frightened or threatened in this rather isolated location - my answer is always in the negative and, anyway, it's not always so quiet up here; just take a walk through the Inclosure on a sunny day especially in the school holidays and you'll be amazed. You'll encounter cyclists, dog walkers, horse riders, carriage drivers, joggers, bird watchers, orienteerers, Duke of Edinburgh awarders, and others just simply enjoying this beautiful Forest of ours. In fact, on occasion, I can stand at my gate and engage person after person in conversation and it's often surprising to learn just how far some individuals have travelled and just how weird is their concept of the New Forest.

I was amused, whilst in a Burley shop, to hear a classic example of this misconception of the Forest. The shopkeeper was asked, by a group of visitors, for directions to the 'forest' and, when she explained that the village was in the Forest, they refused to accept this revelation and advised her that they had been reliably informed that there was, in fact, a specific place called the 'forest'!!

Naturally, I get all sorts of questions up here in the Inclosure. Probably the most common being a request to 'point them in the direction of the car park'. When I ask which particular car park they want they're surprised to learn that there's more than one!

Many see my remote property as a source of information and succour. More often than not people are just lost and, if their map reading skills and sense of direction is anything to go by, that's not surprising! When night is falling many of these are, clearly, frightened and I always ensure that I do everything possible to allay their fears and, if necessary, finish up by reuniting them with their vehicle in some distant car park. On occasion, but fortunately not often, people get injured and they unerringly home-in to my house for help. I have been presented with both broken arms and broken legs, sustained by falling off bicycles on the loose gravel, which has meant calling an ambulance but, up here, that in itself, is no simple matter; you see their modern navigation systems do not recognise my postcode!   Apart from the lost and the injured there are enumerable visitors who are hungry and thirsty and, sometimes, those who just want to use the loo!

Like it or not, we are now in a National Park and that's not going away nor are the tourists who, in some respects, are good for the area, and as one wise old Forester told me 'We didn't want the National Park but now it's here it's no good fighting it, we've got to learn to live with it'.

Education is the name of the game and it's up to us to gently steer these visitors around to our Forests' way of thinking.

Must go now, there's someone at the gate!

July

They're back! They may be late, but they're back! I speak of course of my swallows. They were first spotted about two weeks ago; I had just arrived home from a difficult day on the river bank (you don't believe that, do you?) when I was delighted to hear the unmistakable *tswitt, tswitt, tswitt* of a swallow. Immediately, I headed for the stable yard and, as I passed by the open door of the first loose-box, a blue and white streak shot past my nose and hurtled skywards where it was joined by a second bird. Clearly, these recent arrivals who, as they chased after and called to each other in the evening sky, were celebrating the end of their momentous flight from Africa, I can't be sure, of course, that this is the same pair that came to stay last summer. If it is then they do seem to be more people -tolerant than they were in 2009. The previous birds were very nervous of any human presence and would take flight and disappear at the slightest disturbance; whilst these incumbents fly in and out of the stables with complete disregard to anyone who might be around.

After a few days of hectic activity and much coming and going I was puzzled by the complete lack of nesting progress. Time after time, I peeped over the half-doors expecting to see the rudiments of a new nest under construction or, perhaps, a few mud splatters on the floor – but nothing! Eventually, my ageing brain recalled my 'mirror-on-a-stick'; a little gadget I'd made the year before in order to follow their progress – but where had I put it? The ageing brain struggled in vain with this question and a search of the outbuildings was necessary. It was, of course, hanging on the nails in the lean-to, alongside the garden rake and the digging fork – where else, I ask you, would one hang a 'mirror-on-a-stick'? Anyway, enough of that! The 'mirror-on-a-stick' revealed all and solved the mystery in an instant for there, in the very first nest that was ever built under my roof and which must be at least three or four years old, were three, brown-spotted, eggs. The cogs in the ageing brain turned with a speed that was indicative of approaching senility as it slowly dawned on me that, as a result of the very hot and dry weather conditions we were experiencing, mud, which is the swallows building cement, was in short supply. But did this prevent my enterprising birds from creating a home for their intended family? Oh no, they left their trowels in their tool bag

19

and gave the old domicile a good clean out followed by a snazzy re-lining job and there it was - a nest as good as any you've ever seen and at far less cost. A good example of recycling, I'd say. Wouldn't you?

The three eggs are now five and I wait patiently, but not as patiently as the bird that broods them, for the arrival of the new chicks.

I had another visitor today. It was 6.00 am and, in a semi conscious state, I was preparing the dog food. I was reaching down into the deep and nearly empty feed bin when a sudden movement in the bottom of the container startled me. Now, fully awake, I peered into the bright and beady eyes of an opportunist and very stout wood mouse. I don't know who was more surprised, the mouse, who had tumbled into an inescapable but nutritious trap, or me. Without thinking I opened the door and tipped the bin on its side. The mouse jumped out just as three hungry dogs appeared around the corner. I can reassure you that the mouse beat them to the sanctuary of the shrubbery but it was a close call and I bet he lost some weight in the process!

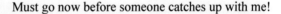

Must go now before someone catches up with me!

Old Swallow Nest in Stables

August

About twenty feet from the kitchen window there hangs, from a gallows bracket attached to a fence post, a peanut feeder. It has been there for many years and birds of every description come to sample the contents of this wire cage whilst several other, less agile species, ferret around beneath the feeder for the tiny morsels of nuts that fall to the ground. A long time ago I placed a railway sleeper at the bottom of the fence, the purpose of which was to deter the 'Escape from Colditz ' attempts of a then, much younger, Jack Russell who took great pleasure, at that time, in digging out.

Recently, a small, round hole appeared, as if by magic, under the sleeper and, at first, I was sure that a bank vole had taken-up residence - but I was wrong. I was standing at the kitchen sink watching the comings and goings of the birds when I was aware of a movement in the foliage below the feeder and there, gathering up the gleanings from the birds above, was a wood mouse. As I watched it stood up on its hind legs and sniffed the air with its long, whiskered nose; the orange, brown fur on its back was in contrast to the pure white belly and the tapering tail was as long again as its body. Then, suddenly, from the aforementioned hole emerged four more tiny, grey mice; clearly the off-spring of the one I was observing. They scurried around at great speed harassing the chaffinches and hedge sparrows that were feeding there. I was mesmerised by their antics and watched for longer than I should have done. Occasionally they would be alarmed by something unseen by me and would dash headlong into their hole only to reappear a few minutes later, when they would jump en-masse to mug some poor, unsuspecting sparrow.

Some time later in the day I remembered the mouse family as I walked past the border and I glanced in the direction of the hole; gone was the tiny, round hole and in its stead was the rotund rump of a frantically digging Jack Russell. He was doing a fair impersonation of a JCB as he scrabbled and scraped at the base of the sleeper and I did not dissuade him – it would have been a waste of breath anyway and I didn't really want the mice to move into the house when the weather got colder.

In fact, they didn't move into the house they moved into my workshop! Wherein is a large, clear-plastic bin that is used for storing the peanuts. I first noticed the presence of the mice when one, much to my amazement, popped its head through a neatly gnawed hole in the plastic bin lid. And that was not all, I lifted the lid and two more leapt like kangaroos over the side and scurried away among the tins of paint on a nearby shelf. I cursed to myself and resolved to repair the hole which, of course, I did not get around to! I wish I had, for an hour or so later, I went back into the workshop to find the bin on its side and three very happy dogs hovering-up the peanuts which were scattered all over the floor.

I suspect that one of them, probably the big, black Labrador, had spotted the mice inside the clear-sided bin and had knocked it over in an attempt to get at them. I righted the bin and, in order to prevent any further mishaps, I placed a large bowl of wood screws onto the lid to weigh it down. What happened next? I think you may have already guessed. I returned some time later to find an upturned bin, yet again, with not only peanuts everywhere but hundreds of screws too!

Must go before you think I'm going screwy too!

Mouse in the Border

September

What a hectic time of year this is. Just lately life seems to gallop away with unrelenting haste. On Friday we travelled up to Ragley Hall for the Game Fair; on the Saturday I had a corporate fishing day; followed on Tuesday, Wednesday and Thursday with 'have a go at fly fishing' at the New Forest Show – and how nice it was to meet so many of you there. The next day, Friday, saw another corporate fishing day and then on the Saturday, guess what! A Druid wedding!! Yes, a Druid wedding or 'Handfasting' which was a very pleasant affair with lots of flowers, bells, food and, of course, liquid refreshment! After this period of non-stop, hectic activity we took a day off and what did we do? We went fishing!!

This manic period when each day started just after dawn and finished well after sunset meant that normal, everyday chores were put on the backburner and when, eventually, I was able to find the time to take a stroll down the garden, I was in for a shock. Despite the abnormally hot and dry weather that we had been enjoying, the lawn had decided to pooh-pooh these arid conditions and had continued to grow until it was now in dire need of a haircut! As I walked past the stables I was looking behind at the unkempt lawn and making a mental note to get the mower out when something grabbed at my shirt sleeve and, at the same time, I felt a sharp tug on my ear. All thoughts of grass cutting vanished as I automatically raised a hand to my ear only to receive a painful jab to my finger. Instantly, the preservation instinct kicked in and I lunged forward, away from this unseen assailant, straight into the unrelenting barbs of a bramble that, during the past few days of no-maintenance on my part, had sent forth, over the fence, several long and sinuous tendrils which dangled in the path of this unsuspecting gardener. Gingerly, I freed my clothing and torn earlobe from the tenacious prickles and at the same time managed to drop my hand into a bunch of nettles that had also taken advantage of my absence and spread into my domain.

I cursed inwardly and went in search of a dock leaf to ease the tingling effect of the nettles; and I didn't have to look far, for in the kitchen garden I was greeted by an abundance of these broad, leathery leaves. They too had enjoyed a holiday from the hoe and whilst many had popped up between the cabbages and carrots even more peeped at me from among the beans and peas. Mother Nature it seems doesn't take time off and, when some of us do, we have to be prepared to pay the penalty. And I was certainly going to pay over the next day or two!

On a more cheerful note, we've had two unusual sightings up here in the Inclosure. A few days ago there appeared an unusual and gawky bird with an enormous maw of a beak. It was, without doubt, a young cuckoo and a very late young cuckoo at that for cuckoos don't stay for long and have usually all departed by the time that August arrives. Even more surprising were its host parents which appeared to be a pair of chaffinches; perhaps the decline in its more usual hosts such as reed warblers or dunnocks had encouraged some enterprising cuckoo to dump its egg into the nest of an alternative species.

Our second sighting was even more unusual in this day and age. A hedgehog was found wandering across the track in broad daylight and, fearing for its safety, my companion picked it up and after tickling it's tummy for a while placed it in the bracken where, with a wiggle of its spines, it snuffled off about its business.

Must go now before you get prickly too!

Vegetable Garden

October

The Chinese have named 2010 The Year of the Tiger. In the May edition of this magazine I pooh-poohed that and wrote that it should be called The Year of the Toad. I now have to eat my own words for, without doubt, 2010 will be remembered, by many of us, as The Year of the Penny Bun! The Penny Bun or Cep or Porcini, as it is known in France and Italy respectively, is probably the most important, edible fungus in the Northern hemisphere and, as I write, it's popping-up just about everywhere! All around us the signs are indicating that this year will be a year of great abundance in the Forest. The hedgerows are flaunting their glistening jewels of blackberries, rosehips, and haws and the trees above are groaning under the weight of crops such as sloes, elderberries, acorns and mast. Similar years of abundance are not that unusual - but it has been many a year since we've had such a fantastic crop of Penny Buns.

These robust, meaty mushrooms whose caps are supported on equally robust and bulbous stems are said to resemble the round, brown, penny buns that were a popular feature in the bakery windows of days gone by. This Prince of fungi is much prized on the continent where it can often be found for sale in the markets. It is commonly prepared and eaten in soups, pasta and risotto but, because it retains its unique flavour when dried, it is used commercially in the mass production of mushroom soup.

Although once feared by the majority of English people and, indeed, considered by most to be a pastime for the insane, fungi foraging has seen a massive increase in popularity and this unexpected, natural bounty has encouraged a large number of foragers into this Forest of ours; and good luck to them, I say, for most are sensible and caring people who recognise the dangers of over harvesting and who are content to gather no more than enough for their own needs.

These mushroom hunters can be observed, along the road-side verges and under the forest canopy, prodding and probing with their stick in one hand and clutching their basket in the other. They look quite normal - happy even, as, head-down, they go about their business. Indeed, when wild mushrooms are not in season, your average Fungi Foragers are, generally, normal people like you and me (??) But, just let one tiny mushroom show its cap, and Doctor Jekyll will become Mr. Hyde.

Like the mushrooms themselves they experience an overnight change and turn into secretive, furtive and even downright devious individuals who will stop at nothing to preserve the secrecy of those locations that have proven, over the years, to be fungi-prolific. Ask any seasoned mushroom hunter for the source of the fungi in his basket and you will be treated to a variety of replies. You may well be told that *'it's a risky business and definitely not one for the inexperienced'*. You might be advised, in no uncertain terms, to *'go away'* or, on the other hand, your mushroom hunter might just suffer from selective hearing and ignore you completely! Sadly there are also those out there who can be so deceitful that they will go to any lengths to protect their private stash of fungi; outwardly they will appear to be friendly and encouraging. They will charm you by giving their advice quite freely and give you explicit directions to some part of the Forest **that will be miles away from their most cherished locations!**

It's my cap, it fits me and I'll wear it!

Beefsteak Mushroom

November

I'm not that comfortable around horses. It's not that I don't like them, you understand, but more often than not, they don't like me! I've been told that I've got an 'electric bum'; which to the layman means that whenever I've been foolish enough to climb on the back of one of these four-legged, grass-converters its temperament has immediately changed from that of a docile riding-school 'hack' into that of a bucking bronco from a Wild West rodeo!! You will appreciate that because of the aforementioned affliction I don't have much experience of horse riding – well, I never really got the chance, did I? For each attempt was inevitably short-lived and usually ended up with a somewhat spectacular and unscheduled dismount into or onto something which was either very hard or very unpleasant! And, despite the terrible treatment that has been delivered upon my person by these animals, I really do like horses; but, without the benefit of an annual MOT and the provision of adequate steering and, more importantly, brakes that work when you want them to, I'll stick to my Land Rover as my preferred form of off-road transport.

You may have gathered by now that I'm more of a dog man than a horse man and there are occasions when I have to admire the enthusiasm and, at the same time question the sanity, of those who chose to keep a horse. And I can speak with some experience on this subject for there have, in days of yore, been horses in my ménage and indeed, there is, as I write, a pony in my paddock for which I have the greatest of respect. She's not mine, you understand, and whilst she will stand still and allow her mistress to do whatever she may wish with her, she treats me with the same disdain as the rest of her equine buddies.

Sometimes, when her doting owner is pushed-for-time, I may be asked to remove her rug. No, this is not a wig, nor is it a small form of carpet. It is, in fact, the horsey equivalent of an overcoat. One of a collection of overcoats that, it seems, every horse must have; there are coats for every occasion; light-weight coats, heavyweight coats and even rain coats. And why do they need these coats? I'll tell you why. It's because their proud and caring owners have paid more folding stuff than they could possibly spend on hair-do's in a year for someone else to come along and clip-off all the nice warm coat that the good Lord blessed the horse with in the first place!

Now, these overcoats are fitted around the body of the said equine with various buckles, straps and Velcro fastenings which make the removal of the garment a job for the experienced only! I have often watched as the 'Doting Owner', with a few endearing words, has released the various fixings in a matter of seconds from her motionless pony. Why then, I ask, when it comes to my turn, does the damned animal, when it sees me approaching, toss her head and run to the furthest corner of the field? Or, even worse, she has been known to stand perfectly still until there's only one more strap to undo and then, without warning, she's off around the paddock at full gallop, dragging the rug which, incidentally, cost more than the average family house to buy, until it's ripped and torn beyond recognition!

As I've said before, I'm not comfortable around horses but here in the Forest they're very much a part of our lives and this would be a sorry place without them – but I'm not finished with horses yet!

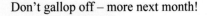

Don't gallop off – more next month!

The Spoilt Pony

December

I may have given you the impression that I don't like horses - well, of course I do. It's just that I have no desire to have one of my own. In my opinion they're too expensive to run; and I quote from experience for I have, in the past, signed countless cheques which were fed into the animal in one way or another and what did I receive in return? Nothing more than an extensive and expensive supply of rhubarb fertiliser, that's what! In fact there are more ways that your equine friend can spend your spare dosh than would fill the entire contents of this esteemed publication.

First and foremost your horse will need a stable; which will inevitably be constructed to the highest (and most expensive) specification. The four-legged lodger will also require a snug bedding of straw from which, on a daily basis, any rhubarb fertiliser, feed and hay which the horse has chosen to scatter over its domain, will be removed. This bedding must then be topped-up with more straw and so the cycle will continue day after day, ad infinitum. Now, straw and hay come in tightly compacted bales which your average horse will consume, in one way or another, at an alarming rate and it makes good economical sense, therefore, to purchase these items in bulk which means the construction of yet another expensive outbuilding called the Hay Barn. Now, here's a little-known fact, (unless you're a horse owner, that is) no matter how much you beat it with a shovel or jump up and down on it, you can never repack your soiled straw into the same dimensions in which it arrived; which leads me nicely to the manure heap, which is a must, and which will start life in a quiet corner of the paddock where it will grow in size at an alarming rate until it has completely engulfed the field and, no matter how many signs you may post at the gate to encourage others to relieve you of the offending stuff, you'll get few takers!

Then, of course, there are the teeth. Great yellow things that, despite continual chewing on costly hay and hard feed, demand, from time to time, the attention of the Equine Dentist! Now anyone who spends the better part of their working day inside the head of a horse, merrily rasping away at the said dentures, deserves, at best, to be sectioned or, at worst, a round of applause. Mind you, once you recover from the shock of his enormous invoice, you'll get some idea of why he does it.

And then, (bear with me - I've nearly finished) there are the shoes. Yes, just in case you didn't know, they wear shoes too. Shoes that cost about half the price of a pair of good, leather brogues; but, unlike brogues, which will last many a year, these shoes, despite being made of metal, will last for a only few weeks. That's when you'll call for the Farrier. Now, to be a farrier was not on my 'what I want to do when I leave school' list, and I'll tell you why. I never, ever, had any ambition to apply a red- hot lump of steel to a horses hoof whilst the said hoof was clasped firmly between my legs, especially with my back to the thinking end of the animal! Nor did I give any thought to then driving several nails into the horses' foot before finishing the job by filing it down with a thumping great rasp!! It's no wonder these shoes are so expensive!

Have a very merry Christmas and feel free to buy me anything but a horse!

Spoilt Pony and Owner with more Expensive Equipment

January

Among all the various animals that I have shared my home with there is one that comes to mind more readily than any other and it might surprise you to know that it wasn't a dog and definitely not a horse! It was a cat and, not just a cat, but an enormous, black and white Tom cat who was, in my opinion, a paragon among cats. Boris was his name and although he had no pedigree to speak of, in my opinion, he was better than any other feline that I've ever known.

Why a paragon among cats I hear you ask and I'll tell you why. Boris was a fanatical 'mouser' - a moggie that never, as far as I know, hunted the birds, which made him very special in my book. It may have been that he was just too idle to pursue the many birds that abounded up here, but I don't think so. It seemed to me that his raison d'être was the pursuit of mice and this he did with a passion. But he wasn't just a killer, like all good country sportsmen who eat whatever they shoot or catch, Boris consumed every mouse that he caught and the store shed and vegetable garden remained relatively mouse-free for many a year.

I said he was enormous but he was fearless too. He treated all dogs with disdain and always stood his ground but only if there was a handy fence or tree in which to seek temporary refuge, if necessary. I recall one February day when we held a lawn meet for the New Forest hounds. There were twenty or so fox hounds mingling about on the track outside and perhaps fifty or more people. Much to the astonishment of the onlookers, Boris wandered through the open gate, sat down on the gravel and proceeded to wash himself with total disregard to the hounds who, it seemed, were too astonished by the cats' attitude to do anything more than stare.

I never, ever, considered that Boris was mine – I didn't own him. In fact, I frequently thought that he owned me! He could be extremely loving but at his own choosing and, despite his occasional feline aloofness, he was a very sociable cat who would always be there to welcome visitors and who was always around when there was a party or a dinner under way. Like all true, males Boris was very fond of the ladies (yes the human kind) and any female who picked him up was rewarded with a cuddle, for the silly great moggie would wrap his front legs around her neck and, purring like a well tuned engine, would nuzzle her face with great enthusiasm.

He was also a great climber which was, on occasion, very nearly his downfall. I once watched him as he climbed, without hesitation, up the ivy on side of the house. When he reached the top he hooked a paw over the guttering to pull himself onto the roof. Unfortunately he slipped and much to my horror he fell two stories to the ground but, to my relief and with a disgruntled shrug, he stalked off unharmed. If a cat could have a sense of humour then Boris did and he often took great delight in running across the roof tiles at night when the resultant din awoke an alarmed house guest on more than one occasion!

Sadly and without warning Boris went to the big hunting ground in the sky and the mice all breathed a sigh of relief - but not me. Quite frankly I missed him and on the basis that I would never find another Boris I vowed that I would not replace him – but, just recently, I did!! I'll tell you about it later.

Have a very happy New Year

Boris

February

To have another cat was not on my 'what I want for Christmas list'. In fact the last thing I wanted was another cat but, surprise, surprise! I've got another cat. I don't really know how this came about – it all happened on the spur of the moment. Somehow I had been lured to the to the 'Cat and Kitten Rescue' where the nice lady said that she had the ideal kitten for me; a kitten of about five months that had been found a few days earlier playing with the traffic on the main road, miles away from any human habitation. She thought that he had probably been 'dumped' on the Forest by his previous owners and, despite this harsh treatment, she said he was a nice, friendly and healthy cat and that he would suit me admirably. I looked at the cat, with his shimmering, jet black fur, a head, a tail and a leg in each corner, he looked alright and I found myself agreeing with her. I knew my resolve was wavering and, in desperation, I blurted out that I had three dogs. She parried this feeble consideration by saying that when introduced to her own dogs, the kitten had shown no fear and was clearly used to being around them. I began to mumble about my garden birds and my furniture and anything else I could think of that would convince her that mine would not be the ideal home for this kitten. She pooh-poohed my reservations and suddenly, as she shoved the feline into a cat basket, I realised that I was doomed. I failed miserably when I tried to think of more reasons for being cat-free and in a dream-like trance I paid a donation to her charity and there you have it! One minute I was happily moggie-free and the next I was walking away from the cat rescue with a cat basket, a litter tray and some food.

Of course I blame the mice. If it wasn't for them and their constant forays into my attic, my workshop and more especially into my kitchen garden where, last year, they managed to decimate almost my entire crop of peas and beans, I wouldn't need a cat – would I?

So, now I have another cat and, in fairness, I have to tell you that he got to work without delay and the mouse population was, within a matter of days of his arrival and despite his diminutive size, being reduced at a good rate of knots. Sadly, the birds have not escaped his attention but I live in hope that he will, like his predecessor, develop a taste for 'red' rather than 'white' meat and that we will be able to coexist in something resembling harmony.

The dogs, I know, are not so sure about this new arrival. Their lives have been disrupted beyond belief but they have shown a stoicism that is, in my opinion, above and beyond the call of duty of any red-blooded canine. Gone now is the Labradors pole position in front of the log fire - the cats got it; gone is the spaniels peaceful sleep after a hard day's work – the cats got her chair; and gone too is the Jack Russell's dignity, apart from an occasional, warning growl that is, as the cat plays with his tail.

In fact the peace that once reigned over my household is no more. This feline is fearless; dogs are pushed off their food, curtains (and legs) are climbed, every cupboard, nook and cranny is explored and the noise of the cat flap, opening and closing incessantly, is a constant irritation. I hope and pray that things will settle down as he matures – that's if he lives that long, of course!

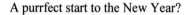

A purrfect start to the New Year?

Sibley

March

Dressing-up is not everyone's cup of tea but it's something that, occasionally, we have to do whether we like it or not. Personally, I'm not a great fan of it and prefer to dress with Comfort rather than Convention as my mentor. But, as with everything, there are exceptions to the rule and where country sports are concerned I'm a real stickler for tradition, which brings me nicely if not a little protractedly to my tale.

The 'Doting Owner' of the pony that lives in the paddock had planned to go hunting on the next meet. This was something she hadn't done for a while and consequently there was much frenzied scurrying, searching and indeed hunting around for all the trappings and paraphernalia that are essential to the well turned-out pony and rider. On the afternoon before the meet, the tack was polished and oiled beyond recognition and the said pony was clipped, scrubbed, generally de-matted and then re- plaited; its hooves were burnished till they glowed and its teeth were polished to a Hollywood smile. Finally, without disturbing a hair, it was carefully tucked–up in its nice warm stable and that, I thought, would be that until the next day; alas how callow could I be, how stupid to imagine that a peaceful and relaxed evening lay ahead. Oh no! Riding boots were polished and bulled to parade ground standard; shirt, stock and jodhpurs were washed and ironed; hat, waistcoat and hunting jacket were duly brushed and stock-pin, flask, crop and watch were laid out in preparation of the big day. And then, thank goodness, to bed.

But not for long! At some ungodly hour the 'Doting Owner' was up and off to the stable to administer to the spoilt pony's needs which, no sooner done, she returned to see to her own. A bath, hair up and netted, make-up on, stock tied and pinned, jodhs, waistcoat and jacket on and, I have to say, she looked like a million dollars.

Before I was out of bed she had gone to saddle-up, an early start was called for. It would take a good hour to hack across the Forest to where the hounds were due to meet and she was determined to be punctual. I arrived in the yard in time to help her mount the pony and after the usual farewells she rode off in the direction of Boldrewood.

About thirty minutes later my fading hearing told me that someone was calling me and, to my amazement, there were the 'Doting Owner' and the pony heading for the stable yard. Fearing the worst, I hurried down the garden and arrived to find her dismounted.

''Just look at Me.'' she wailed.

I did just that and, silly me, I thought she looked fine.

''Just look at my feet.'' she wailed again.I looked down as instructed. Oh dear! Poor girl! Where the beautifully polished riding boots should have been was a pair of disreputable and filthy wellies. In her haste to get to the event she had forgotten to change her footwear. But change them she did and off she set, once again. She never did make the meet nor did she find the hounds, but she had a good four-hour ride which she thoroughly enjoyed; even more so in the knowledge that both she and the spoilt pony were impeccably turned–out.

You see the important thing is that it doesn't matter what state you are in after a day on the Forest. In fact the amount of Forest that you have on or about your person at the end of the day is usually directly proportional to the amount of fun you've had! It's how you appear at the start of the day that matters; it shows that you care for your sport and have respect for its traditions.

Go on! Have some fun! Get muddy!

Lawn Meet at Burley Rails

April

Sell the New Forest or perhaps give it away to a charitable organisation? Never heard such a load of nonsense! What will they think of next? How could anyone in their right sense of mind imagine that the future of somewhere as unique as the New Forest – the crowning glory of the whole Forestry Commission Estate – that has taken hundreds of years to evolve, could be decided by the proposed, twelve-week public consultation?

Here in the Forest, the Government announcement of the intended 'Public Consultation on the Future of the Public Forest Estate' caused a remarkable surge of activity. Within days and after much frantic telephoning, emailing and word-of-mouthing a protest meeting was arranged for 12.00 on Saturday 19th February at Boltons' Bench. The TV, local radio, the press and the politicians were informed; Keepers, Rangers, Commoners, Licencees, Forestry Commission employees, Local and County Councillors and hundreds of other concerned people were expected to attend. But the timing, for us anyway, was not good. That particular Saturday had been designated for our annual lawn meet, when at 10.45 the fox hounds and their followers were due to meet up here in the inclosure for some tasty nibbles and a drop of something liquid and warming before they set-off, as tradition prevailed, to follow the, now false, scent of Charlie fox.

Naturally we wanted to be involved and have our say and the Fox Hounds and their supporters wanted to be present too. We were asked if we could possibly delay our 'meet' until 2.00pm. There followed much more telephoning, emailing and word-of-mouthing and the scene was set. The 'meet' was rescheduled for 2.00pm; some of us would go to the meeting at Lyndhurst whilst others were to remain in the inclosure to hold the fort and to victual anyone who turned up for the cancelled 10.45 'meet'. And then, guess what? Much to everyones' delight, on 17th February the Government withdrew the Public Consultation and, in consequence, threw uncertainty into our agenda. Once again the phone lines buzzed, the ether overheated and over-mouthed mouths dried-up. Would we revert to our normal time of 10.45? Would the planned protest go ahead? Confusion, for a while reigned, but in the event, we stuck to our plans and attended the public meeting and then hurried back to mull the wine for an enjoyable and social lawn meet.

But why, I hear you ask, would we be prepared to go to all this trouble? And I'll tell you why. It's because we who work, live and play in this most beautiful of locations are more aware than anyone else just how important and how sensitive this Forest of ours is in the general scheme of things and we are, naturally, concerned for our and the Forests wellbeing.

In the New Forest, the ecology and the way of life is unique and we are surrounded by generations of specialised and intimate knowledge. Knowledge possessed and passed down through the Forestry Commission workers, the Keepers, the Verderers and their Agisters and countless Commoners who actually know how it all works. It seems senseless, to me anyway, to jeopardise all this wealth of knowhow by handing our Forest over to another amorphous organisation when we have everything we need to hand. We cannot afford to lose what has taken hundreds of years to accumulate. A twelve-week public consultation was never going to be the answer and the considered closure of the Forestry Commission would be a negative step.

The Countryside has won an almost unprecedented victory - for the moment! But we watch this space and wait, with baited breath, for the outcome of the independent panel of 'experts' who are being appointed, as I write, to decide upon our future.

Do watch your backs!

May

Do you remember when we had our own, resident police officer? Our very own Village Bobby who knew most of us, good or not so good, by name; and whose very presence was reassuring to the God-fearing and honest residents of the Forest and a deterrent to those who might be inclined to stray from the straight and narrow. Sadly, it has been many years since Government cutbacks or reorganisation or whatever the reason took away our personal defender of law and order.

I for one don't like the current situation and this was reinforced not so long ago when, late one evening, I had occasion to call the police to report a non-stop, car alarm which was sounding from the direction of Lucy Hill car park. To my amazement I found myself talking to a representative of the Constabulary in Southampton, of all places. I expressed my surprise and it was explained that Ringwood and Lyndhurst police stations are closed after a certain time and that all calls are directed to them. I explained about the vociferous car alarm at Lucy Hill and was informed that the police were very busy and wouldn't it be simpler to phone Lucy Hill herself and ask her to rectify the offending alarm!! I tried to explain that Lucy Hill was a location and not a person but I felt that I would have got more sense by phoning Alcoholics Anonymous than calling the police and, as I replaced the handset, I felt strangely remote and isolated. But all that has changed. We now have, once again, our very own rural police unit. Not dedicated or restricted to our own fair village of Burley, you understand, but committed to reducing crime in the countryside around the New Forest area. It's called Country Watch and is the brainchild of Sergeant Louise Hubble who, with two Police Constables and one Community Support Officer in her team, encourages public participation in the fight against rural crime. Each Officer has been carefully selected and is either from a rural background or has a genuine interest in the countryside. Louise, when off duty, can often be seen in the beating line during the shooting season and is currently training a newly acquired Labrador pup. One of her Officers hails from a long line of gamekeepers and another is a keen countryman and angler. Without exception and not surprisingly, they are all qualified Wildlife Crime Officers, Equine Liaison Officers and Hunt Liaison Officers. Similarly, they are trained animal handlers and can deal with most situations involving farm, domestic and wild animals including birds of prey and sometimes the more exotic creatures such as reptiles and parrots.

In order to reinforce their commitment and to help to spread the word, Hampshire Constabulary organise special events where members of the public are encouraged to become involved with the Country Watch Scheme, which is an essential factor for its on-going future. In addition to these organised events, free advice is offered on subjects such as security and crime prevention and Officers are pleased to visit rural premises to inspect and comment on any issues. They maintain a high profile at events such as country shows, hunt meets, village fetes, etc. when they are often rewarded by invaluable word-of-mouth information from members of the public.

Country Watch is here for us and, contrary to widespread belief, rural crime is, in the eyes of the police, an important issue. But public participation is an essential ingredient to the success of the unit so, take the advice of Louise Hubble and help the police fight rural crime by reporting anything suspicious, no matter how insignificant it may appear. 'Together we can make the rural community a better place to live in'

Keep your eyes peeled!

Country Watch Poster

June

According to the RSPB the Cuckoo, that well known harbinger of spring, is in serious decline, which you would find difficult to believe if you lived up here in the Inclosure. They seem to be everywhere. Indeed, since the 7th April, when the fist bird was heard, we have been the recipients of a continual cacophony of cuckooing. Even as I write in mid May their unique calls are echoing around the Forest from dawn until dusk. Now I have to say that this was not the case in the spring of 2010 when the call of the cuckoo really was an infrequent sound. I wish I could explain the reason for what seems to be an amazing recovery in status - but I can't. Perhaps the unusually warm and dry weather has got something to do with it - who knows?

The sound of the Cuckoo always makes me smile and reminds me of a tale that I read many years ago. A couple, fed-up with the Rat-Race of city life, had taken the plunge and changed their lifestyle completely by giving up their well paid jobs and moving to a remote village in Norfolk, where they took over the general store and post office. Communication was an immediate problem; particularly with the older inhabitants whose beautiful Norfolk accents fell strangely onto their unpractised ears. One day, this husband and wife were busily serving customers when into the store came an elderly lady who walked directly up to the man and looking him straight in the eye said "Cuckoo". "Cuckoo?" he replied with a puzzled look on his face. "Cuckoo" she replied with a knowing nod. In desperation he looked round at the other customers for help. A housewife, seeing his predicament, came to his rescue. "Cuckoo" she said. He looked to his wife for help but she only shrugged her shoulders and shook her head as the other customers joined in. "Cuckoo, Cuckoo" resounded all around the shop. "It must be a plot to drive us mad" he whispered to his wife. Then one helpful and younger lady went to a shelf and taking down an item handed it to the elderly customer who, in turn, banged the tin of cocoa! down on the counter in front of the shopkeeper and pointing to it said "Cuckoo!"

Seriously though, this is a most extraordinary start to the year and at the time of writing it has been many weeks since we had any rain to speak of and the temperatures have, on occasion, exceeded any previous recordings. In consequence many of the things around us are far more advanced than they were last spring. The trees are in full leaf which they certainly weren't at the same time of year in 2010 and many species of birds are nesting much earlier than before. The St Georges mushroom, which generally occurs on St Georges Day on 23rd April, obligingly and surprisingly popped-up at the beginning of that month and provided us with some very tasty breakfasts. Less popular, I'm sure, and something that has been missing for several years up here, are the May Bugs or Cockchafers those big, brown beetles with spiky legs which crash into the windows with such a thump and which have, like the Cuckoo, returned in abundance and in mid April too!

Equally unpopular with some of us are bees, especially when they chose to swarm in our gardens. I've had several calls this year from worried residents who've been surprised and frightened by the sight of a huge, buzzing mass of insects suspended from their tree and, although I could not give much help at the time, I now have the contact details for a bee keeper who will gladly come and remove them.

Must buzz off now before you get waspish with me!

St Georges Mushroom

July

To have a phobia or a fear of anything is not pleasant. My own particular Waterloo is a fear of heights. I remember a time, many years ago, when I was capable of scaling anything but, I'm afraid to say, that as the great wheel of life has turned, my ability to climb has diminished. Indeed, these days it takes great effort and supreme willpower to clamber onto the dizzying heights of a bar stool; but somehow I manage!!

Phobias can take many forms and can, sometimes, be the source of untypical behaviour; an instance of which was related to me recently by a very distraught lady. There was, staying with us, a nice, young couple. She had arrived with a fine-boned, grey, mare, which showed all the signs of some Arab bloodline. It was apparent from the outset that she loved this animal as only a girlie can love a horse. Her husband, on the other hand, displayed totally different feelings where the beast was concerned. He expressed a deep mistrust of anything equine and resolutely avoided the aforementioned mare and avoided the Forest ponies with such consummate caution that it soon became apparent that he was possessed of a severe phobia of anything to do with four-legged grass-converters. His raison-d'être, however, was a mountain bike; it was his pride and joy and he drooled over and polished this amalgam of rubber and steel with as much passion as his attractive spouse showed when grooming her beloved horse.

Despite their differences over choice of steed they were obviously devoted to each other and, on their respective and very different 'mounts', they were able to enjoy their time in the Forest and rode out together as often as they could. Their euphoric existence continued for several days until, unfortunately, they came upon a situation that was to test their love for each other; an ordeal that could have ended in tears!

There was, not far from the cottage a fine, black and lusty New Forest stallion that, having assembled an entourage of mares, had herded them into the relative privacy of our Inclosure. On the fateful day in question the devoted pair, whilst riding along the track, he on his shining bike and she on her shining mare, came upon the stallion and his ladies. Whether it was through ignorance or innocence, I don't know, but the youngsters failed to notice that one of the ponies in the herd was constructed in a different way to the others. The stallion, however, recognised the mare for what she was and fell passionately in love with her and decided to add her to his harem.

The woman, who had been around horses for many a year, snapped out of her reverie as she recognised that the rapidly approaching pony was indeed a stallion; not just a stallion but a stallion whose demeanour suggested trouble! She shouted a warning to her loved-one and suggested that he should 'shoo-away' the fast-approaching beast. Alas, she heard no response from her husband and turned her mare in time to see her would-be rescuer, half-hidden in a cloud of dust, peddling furiously in the opposite direction!

As luck would have it, at that very moment, the stallion was distracted by the sight of a pretty, brown-eyed, Forest filly that trotted into his path and any feelings that he had for the slender Arab dissolved away as he abruptly and obediently followed this new love into the trees.

I know that editorial pruning would certainly not allow me to relate, word for word, the berating that our young man received from his wife when she caught up with him! But, take it from me, she was not best pleased!!

Love, it seems, that should conquer all, on this occasion, didn't!

New Forest Ponies

August

There are times when I think my ramblings should be headed 'From the Madhouse' rather than 'From the Inclosure' And, before any of you make any comment about my personal sanity, it's the quirky animals that I'm sharing my abode with that are giving cause for concern, not me! Let me explain.

Assuming that your powers of recall are better than mine, you might just remember that in the February edition of this erudite publication I told you about the addition of a cat to my ménage. This cat, I have to tell you is, quite frankly, bonkers. You see, he thinks he's a dog – not just any old dog, you understand, but the dominant dog – he acts as if he is the leader of the pack and my silly mutts go along with him! When, occasionally, the dogs rouse themselves from their beds and decide to have a game of chase around the garden, the cat will be there too and in true canine fashion he will join in the pursuit; twisting and turning and being bowled over with the best of them until he, the cat that is, has had enough. Similarly, when we take a walk in the Forest the cat will be there and, more often than not, he will be striding-out in front of the rest of the pack; stopping once in a while to conceal himself in the bracken from whence he will pounce on the poor-old, unsuspecting pooches!

But the cat's not the only mad inhabitant. We've got chickens that think they're human! I'm not exaggerating they really do! They arrived a few weeks ago from one of those new-age farms where children are encouraged to handle and feed the animals and consequently, should anyone hove in sight they'll descend, en-masse, to see what, if anything, is on offer. And should you be so bold as to sit down on the patio with a cup of tea and a sandwich then you'd better be quick; for when I tried it they were on me in a flash and whilst the sandwich disappeared before my very eyes, the tea ended up in my lap! They have invaded the conservatory, the kitchen and the laundry room but I had to put my foot down when I found three of them on the back of the settee in the sitting room (no pun intended!)

And then, of course, there's the pony that thinks it's a chicken! The chickens are free-range but they do have, attached to their house, a little wire run which is about 9'0" long, 4'0" wide and 6'0" high. In the end of this caged structure is a narrow door with a step-over at the bottom where the wire has been buried deeply to deter the attention of Mr. Charlie Fox. The door is left open so that when the hens are being hen-like and not humanoid they can go in and out at their leisure. Just recently, during this dry spell, the pony has been allowed to graze the lawn, which, I'm pleased to say, saves me a lot of mowing. You can imagine my surprise when I noticed, the other day, that the pony had managed to squeeze into this tiny chicken run and was dozing quite peacefully in the confined space. The doting owner was summoned and to my amazement and great concern she promptly climbed into the cage with the stupid equine. I expressed concern for her safety and, thankfully, I cannot put into print her response. Nor can I publish her scathing retort when I refused, point-blankly, to lift the pony's rear feet over the aforementioned step-over. However, despite my abject fear of the back-end of any horse I did as I was told and, like a cork from a bottle, the pony popped out of the run and reverted to being a sane animal, once again.

Must go before you think I'm mad too!

The Spoilt Pony in the Chicken Run

September

The hot, dry weather continues with very little respite. Recently we've been cooked at the Game Fair and roasted at the New Forest Show! This morning, the inanely, smiling weather man promised temperatures of up to 30 degrees (or 86 degrees in old money!) clearly, he doesn't grow his own vegetables or he wouldn't have worn that stupid grin!

Across the Country, children have just been released from school for their long summer holidays and, no doubt, this warm and sunny weather will bring many newcomers to this lovely Forest of ours. And, whilst on the subject of newcomers, I can tell you that we've had, already, two new arrivals, up here in the Inclosure – one very welcome and the other definitely not!

A few days ago, whilst weeding the kitchen garden and inwardly cursing the tenacity of these unwanted invaders that, despite these torrid conditions, are threatening to engulf my vegetables, I heard a bird song that was unfamiliar. A delicate, liquid twittering was coming from somewhere above and it didn't take more than a few seconds to locate the source of this most pleasant of sounds. There on the very top of a nearby tree, singing its heart out, was a cock goldfinch; one of our most striking birds with its plumage of black, white, brown and yellow and a bright, red face-patch it is easily identified but not, I must say, a common bird of the forests. These stunning little creatures are usually found on waste ground or meadows where they hang like blue tits from the seed heads of thistles, teasels and hawkweeds. As I watched and enjoyed this tiny bird I became aware of several more that were feeding in the surrounding trees and so, you see, I was privileged to have, albeit for a short while, a 'charm' (for this is their collective noun) of goldfinches in the Inclosure!

But not every new visitor is welcome! I found a dead rat on the lawn – yes, a rat! Not a creature that anyone welcomes around their home and one that has rarely been spotted up here. I assumed that the new cat (the one that thinks it's a dog) had brought it in from the surrounding Forest. You can imagine my surprise when the very next day I found another in exactly the same spot and just as dead. I wandered down to the stable yard to report my finding to the doting-owner of the spoilt pony who was, indeed, spoiling the pony as I arrived. As I was relating my discovery I noticed, on some seed trays containing French Marigolds, several mice that appeared to be a bit wobbly. I pointed these out to my partner and she asked me what they were; and after little delibertion it became obvious that these were, in fact, young rats and no doubt the off -spring of the two corpses that I had found on the lawn.

Clearly they had to go, but they were too small to trap and too wary to catch. I did the next best thing and shot a couple with the little .410 shotgun; after which the survivors took cover in the wood shed and refused to re-show. I couldn't waste valuable time by waiting for them so I returned to my work leaving my partner to finish the job. It wasn't long before I was pleased to hear the modest report from the little gun and I hurried down the garden to see the outcome. I was amazed to find her collecting and re-planting marigolds that had been scattered far and wide! You see, although she had bagged two rats with one cartridge she'd shot them whilst they were among the marigold seedlings - with devastating results!

I'm so glad that it wasn't me that had transplanted her seedlings in such a way – it would have been a different story then, I can tell you!

Must go before I get shot too!

October

Did you go to the village show this year? I did – well, actually, I was threatened with unmentionable consequences if I didn't go – so I had to, didn't I? In recent years I've avoided the show for no other reason than I couldn't be bothered. Traditionally, I always attend the bigger shows such as the CLA Game Fair, the New Forest Show, the Shaftesbury and Gillingham Show and the Great Dorset Steam Fair so what on earth could the Burley Village Show offer a battle-hardened, show veteran like myself? Well, in retrospect, I can tell you that it gave me a few hours of fun and an immense amount of enjoyment and satisfaction.

It all started when the doting owner of the spoilt pony came home, back in July, with the show schedule and began at once to tick-off those classes that she thought she should enter. (I must point out before I go any further that 'she', on this occasion, should generally be interpreted as 'we'!!). Quite frankly, I thought the woman had gone mad. She seemed to be putting a tick beside nearly every class. I tried to reason with her but I knew, when I saw the competitive gleam in her eyes, that I was wasting my time. There was nothing I could do but, reluctantly, to do as I was told and 'join in the fun'. And, in the event, it did turn out to be terrific fun and I'm only sorry that I hadn't been involved in previous years.

On the morning of the Show 'she'- not 'we', you understand, had to be elsewhere so it was left to 'me'-not 'us'- to deliver and display the entries. I have to admit that I was apprehensive about our first attempt on the show bench but no sooner had I arrived than I realised that I knew many of the people who were there, in fact, several were old friends. An air of friendly rivalry dominated the occasion but this did not deter some kindly help and advice. Cling film, a requirement on foodstuff, which I didn't have, was provided by a generous adversary and I thank her very much.

At one o'clock we arrived and duly paid our entry fee of £1.00 each! A far cry from the double-figure charges of the bigger shows. I was immediately taken aback by the number of people who were flocking into the show but as we wandered around I could see just what had attracted over two thousand visitors; there was something for everyone. Rural crafts, vintage cars, a falconry display, a well attended dog show and much, much more.

Having had a good look around the show we joined the throng of people who were eagerly inspecting the judges' decisions and comments in the various show tents. Again, I was pleased to see that here too there was something for everyone; classes for vegetables, flowers, pot plants, home-made produce, photography and knit and stitch. And, as for the younger people, they had their classes too.

We were pleasantly surprised to see how well she had done in the showing and although the prize money was less than the price of a celebratory drink it didn't matter. What did matter was being a part of the community and taking part in this fun, fund raising event; an event that proved to be a credit to all the hard working individuals who helped to organise and manage the day. So, if you didn't attend with the two thousand or so who did, just make sure that you do so in 2012 and more than that, whilst you're at it, do enter one or two classes in the show as well . You might be astounded by the results.

I know she/we were!

Success at the Village Show

November

Our beautiful Forest is under threat once again. A Forestry Commission review group, in an attempt to help the Government trim down the number of Civil Servants by twenty-five percent, has recommended a reduction in New Forest Keepers. They are, in fact, proposing that the Keeper team be reduced to just seven Beat Keepers.

It goes without saying that this bombshell has given every incumbent Keeper cause for considerable concern not only over his own future but over the future of the unique environment that is the New Forest. A New Forest Keeper is not just another Civil Servant with a job to do; he is vocational, passionate about his responsibilities and possesses a unique and specialised knowledge of his working environment.

No one could be more qualified to report on the impact of a reduction in the number of Keepers than the Keepers themselves and yet, despite repeated requests to be directly involved with the review, the Keepers have been ignored.

Since the advent of the New Forest National Park we have all been aware of a huge increase in the number of visitors. At the same time budgetary constraints have resulted in a gradual decline in the integrity of the infrastructure. Dragons' teeth, gates, barriers and road-side ditches that were built to protect the Forest are rotting or falling into disrepair, and illegal vehicular access is damaging the very fabric of the Forest and increasing our Keepers workload. The New Forest is, in the global scheme of things, a very important and sometimes fragile environment and if it is to remain so then these visitors, who have every right to and are, indeed, encouraged to come and visit this unique part of England, need to be educated, guided and controlled and it's difficult to imagine how this will be achieved without the Keepers to continue with this vital role.

One of the principal functions of a Keeper is to manage and cull the deer and years of experience indicate that a minimum of ten skilled marksmen, with the ability and knowledge to work alone, are required to achieve the annual quota. Our Keepers have carried out this duty with such care and awareness to public safety that few of you are ever conscious of their presence. We need then to continue their good work for whilst there are deer on the Forest they will always need to be managed and, as a stalker myself, I don't relish the thought of outside contractors doing this sensitive job.

New Forest Keepers fulfil their duties on a weekly roster and, collectively, they provide and maintain twenty-four hour cover. For health and safety, loan-working and beat coverage reasons they also work in pairs. How this will all be possible if their numbers are reduced to just seven is anybody's guess.

Whilst no one doubts that this country is in trouble and that the Civil Service could do with a bit of pruning, can this recommendation be in the best interests of the nation? I don't think so! The New Forest is known as the Jewel in the Crown of our national forests and the Crown Keepers believe that they cannot effectively protect the New Forest if their numbers are reduced to less than ten.

Retirement and relocation have already reduced the current Keeper team to just one Head Keeper and nine Beat Keepers. Will the loss of three more members of the team have that much effect on the nations finances? One thing is certain, the New Forest is under threat and always will be and if the Crown Keepers aren't there to look out for it then who will?

'If it 'aint broke, don't mend it'!

New Forest in the Snow

December

Not so long ago, I was in the bar of one of the more remote Forest pubs when it dawned on me just how quickly things change. The bare, wooden floor boards and the room, generally, hadn't altered that much, over the years; but the rest of the building had been transformed quite dramatically and the numerous tables that were placed in every conceivable location left no doubt, that the foremost purpose of this refurbished drinking-house was the provision of food. The customers, too, were different; cyclists, ramblers, campers and tourists but not a single 'local' among them. I wondered what they might have thought had they been in the same room, on a certain evening, some thirty years before.

The bar was crowded on the evening that came to mind. With few exceptions they were Forest people and most of them were Commoners who each had varying numbers of beasts on the Forest. The landlord, a congenial giant, who was himself a Commoner, announced in the general conversation that he reckoned he had the smallest foal on the Forest, that year. In typical Forest fashion, this statement was countered and derided by claims and sightings of smaller beasts in other ownership. The conversation drifted on to other topics and was forgotten until, about twenty minutes later, the side door was kicked open and in came the aforementioned landlord carrying, in his arms, the tiniest of foals, whilst close on his heels followed a concerned and diminutive Shetland mare

He placed the little animal on the wooden floor for all to see and stood back in triumph. The worried mare stood protectively by her offspring and looked, threateningly, about her. Meanwhile, the pub dog, roused by all the commotion, ventured-out from under a settle and sniffed, tentatively, at the minuscule foal. The feisty mare spotted the dog and, turning her rear end in its direction, she lashed out with her heels narrowly missing the cur but sending an old table and the glasses thereon, flying. Suddenly, all hell broke loose; the dog retaliated by snapping at the mare which, in turn, tried similar tactics and with great, yellow teeth attempted to latch onto her antagonist.

After much yelling and cursing the animals were eventually evicted and tables and chairs were up righted. A sense of normality began to return and I watched as a tourist, who had observed the unusual spectacle, came up the bar carrying two, empty, pint mugs.

"That was amazing" he said, as he placed the glasses on the bar. "You wouldn't see anything like that in my local, I can tell you. Fill 'em up again, please, landlord." And pointing at one of the mugs he added. "I wonder if you wouldn't mind changing that glass?"

The landlord, always ready for a laugh, took his time and, having scrutinised the glass with great care, replied. "What's the matter with 'un?"

The unwary stranger turned and pointed to the dog, which had retreated to its place under the settle, and replied for all to hear. "Well, I spotted that dog having a drink from it."

The gentle giant leaned over the bar and made an exaggerated inspection of the mangy dog. He winked at me before he straightened up and then, looking the stranger sternly in the eye, he nodded to the glass in his hand and asked. "An' tell me. Was this glass yours?"

The bar fell silent as everyone listened to his tremulous reply. "Y'yes, it was."

"Well, I hope my dog's all right then." Grinned the landlord as he turned to fill the glasses, amidst the roars of laughter from the locals.

Hope your Christmas is all right then! Have a good one.

The other books From a New Forest Inclosure

From A New Forest Inclosure
The First Two Years
Ian Thew

From a New Forest Inclosure
Book Two 2006 & 2007
Ian Tew

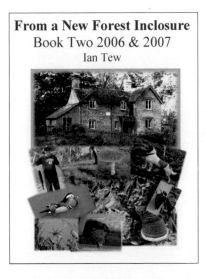

From a New Forest Inclosure
Book Three 2008 & 2009
Ian Thew

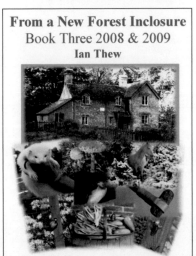

From A New Forest Inclosure
Book Four 2010 & 2011
Ian Thew

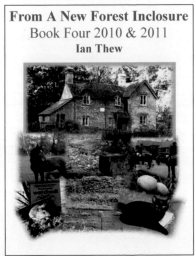

These books are available by post: Please send £5,99 per book plus £2.50 postage and packaging (up to four books) to Ian Thew, Burley Rails Cottage, Burley BH24 4HT England Or telephone 01425 403735 with your name, postal address and card details. Email ian@ithew.freeserve.co.uk

Burley Rails Cottage, Wilfs Cabin and Paddocks

Wilfs Cabin

Stables

Wilfs Cabin; a self-contained, snug, traditional log cabin that provides a double bed room with en-suite shower, a cosy lounge and a galley kitchen. The timbered veranda is ideal for alfresco dining or for just relaxing with a glass of wine after a busy day in the Forest.

For the four legged visitors there are two, modern, block-built, stables with individual yards and a tack room with all facilities, which are adjacent to two small turn-out paddocks. There is ample parking and undercover storage for traps and bikes.

www.burleyrailscottage.co.uk   Tel:01425 403735

Well behaved and sociable dogs are also welcome.

NEWF⊕REST
Shooting & Fishing | Coaching & Tuition

The New Forest Fly Fishing and Shooting School was founded by Ian Thew who lives deep in the heart of the New Forest which is situated on the South Coast between the mighty rivers Test and Avon and offers the ultimate in fishing and shooting possibilities.

Our objective is to provide the very best in fly fishing and clay and game shooting for both the complete novice or the experienced sportsman and to this end we extend the opportunity to learn new skills or to hone existing expertise over a wide range of disciplines.

We take pride in providing instruction and coaching in all aspects of fishing and shooting to the very highest of standards and we take care to ensure that when our pupils leave us they will have been well versed in both safety and etiquette and will thus be able to move on in their selected sport with personal assurance and confidence.

Ian Thew is a qualified fly fishing coach and a qualified shooting instructor and, in addition to running the New Forest Fly Fishing and Shooting School, he writes regular features on all aspects of shooting, fishing and country sports related topics for magazines such as the Shooting Times and the Countrymans' weekly.

Ian is also a qualified deer stalker and over the past forty years he has amassed a unique and widespread knowledge of most rural activities from fishing to ferreting and just about everything else in between.

Contact Ian on 01425 403735 or email ian@ithew.freeserve.co.uk

www.shootingandfishingcoaching.co.uk